M000006579

CCSS Genre Drama

Essential Question
How do you decide what is important?

THE NAMING OF
ATHENS
A PLAY

by Dawn McMillan
illustrated by Maxim Larin

THE NAMING OF ATHENS

Characters

Reader

Cecrops *(SEE-krahps)*, a half-man, half-serpent, who will be the king of the new city

Gods and Goddesses of Olympia, including:

Zeus, king of the gods

Poseidon *(puh-SIGH-duhn)*, god of the sea

Athena, goddess of wisdom

Citizen One

Other Citizens

List of Props

Poseidon's trident, a large rock, water jars, an olive seed, an olive tree

Scene One
The New City

On a rocky hilltop in ancient Greece

READER: Athens was the most powerful city in ancient Greece. The people of this city had a civilization that is still admired today. This is how the city got its name.

CECROPS: (*to the gathered gods and goddesses*) Gods and goddesses of Olympus, here we are high on this hilltop, and see there below us, our beautiful land. Of course I've named the land after myself, Cecrops. And now I see the beginnings of a new city—a beautiful city. It seems right that the new city should be called Cecrops as well.

GODS AND GODDESSES: (*together*) No! No! We want to name this new city after one of us. Call it after me!

No, me!

The city should have *my* name.

I'll name the city.

POSEIDON: Listen, my friends! The city should have my name. After all, I am Poseidon, god of the sea, and everyone knows how powerful the ocean is. This city reaches to the sea. Yes! The city should be called Poseidon. Poseidon! Now that is a great name for a new city in our beloved land.

ATHENA: Perhaps not, Poseidon. I can see that you are obsessed with the idea of the city having your name, but maybe it's not such a good idea. The sea can be wild and angry. Perhaps the city should have a quieter name, like mine. After all, I am the goddess of wisdom, and the people in our new city will need to be wise.

POSEIDON: Absolute nonsense. I…

ZEUS: Wait! My friends, this squabbling will only bring us anguish. Poseidon, Athena, I can see that you both have strong feelings about this. Each of you wants the city named after you, and both of you have a good claim. Let me think. I need to find a way to decide between you. I will ask thunder for help.

Thunder rolls loudly.

ZEUS: Gods and goddesses, do not be alarmed! The thunder has great wisdom. Poseidon and Athena, you will each bring a gift for the city. Tomorrow we will all meet here again on this hilltop, and you will show us what you have brought. If you bring the best gift, you will have the city named after you.

GODS OF OLYMPUS: (*together*) Good idea! Bring us your gifts then. Tomorrow we shall decide.

ZEUS: Ah, but I think it's necessary for the citizens to see the gifts that Poseidon and Athena bring. I will send a rainbow to lead them to this place.

GODS OF OLYMPUS: Yes!

Of course!

The citizens must agree!

Rightly so!

Fair enough!

The citizens must be consulted!

The citizens must decide!

ZEUS: Until tomorrow, then.

Scene Two
The Gods' Gifts

READER: The next day the citizens of the city and the gods of Olympus gathered together on the hilltop.

CECROPS: Welcome! Welcome! Come, make yourselves comfortable. Oh, there you are, Zeus. Here, sit by me. A very good morning it is this morning. Just a little shower earlier, for your rainbow. Now the sun is shining brightly, and it is a good day indeed for deciding the name of our new city.

ZEUS: Greetings, all. Gods, goddesses, citizens... we are meeting here today to view the gifts that Poseidon, god of the sea, and Athena, goddess of wisdom, have prepared for our city. The first to present his gift is... Poseidon! Welcome, Poseidon!

Poseidon steps forward and bows. Everyone claps.

POSEIDON: Behold! I possess great powers. See the magic that happens when I strike this rock with my trident!

Poseidon marches forward, strikes a large rock, and then turns to face the citizens.

See how the water gushes from the rock! Citizens of the new city, I bring you a never ending supply of water. Never again will your crops wither and die in the hot summer sun. Never again will you go thirsty. This gift of mine is a miracle. It is what the city needs!

CITIZEN 1: Poseidon, a never ending supply of water is, indeed, a miracle. Fresh water, you say?

POSEIDON: Of course! It is fresh, clean water. Taste it for yourselves!

CITIZEN 1: Ugh! This water tastes terrible! It's salty, like the sea!

CITIZENS: (*tasting the water*) Ugh!

Dreadful!

Disgusting!

Undrinkable!

CITIZEN 1: Poseidon, the sea fills our water jars. No! No! This will not do! This water is not a suitable gift for our city.

The citizens shake their heads, screw up their faces, and pour the water from their jars.

CECROPS: Indeed, it will not do!

ZEUS: Oh dear! Poseidon, your power as god of the sea is too strong. Strike the rock again and stop the flow of this salty water immediately!

Poseidon strikes the rock and leaves the stage angrily.

CITIZENS: Athena! Athena! We want Athena!

ZEUS: Yes. Athena, please come forward and show us your gift.

Athena comes to stand in front of the citizens and gods and goddesses, and everyone waits in anticipation.

ZEUS: (*looking puzzled*) Your gift, Athena. Where is your gift?

Athena opens her hand to show an olive seed. She turns to face the citizens.

ATHENA: Here it is, my citizens. Here is my gift for your city. This will give you food and oil to cook with. This will give you firewood to keep you warm in winter. These things are necessary for a good life in our new city. Watch as I plant this seed.

The citizens and the gods and goddesses gather around as Athena plants the seed in the ground.

ATHENA: See how the seed grows!

An olive tree prop is pushed onto the stage.

GODS AND GODDESSES: Ohhh! A miracle!

CITIZENS: Incredible!

Everyone claps.

CITIZEN 1: This is a great gift, one we need. It will bring our city wealth. Athena, we must name the city after you.

CITIZENS: Athena! Athena! Athena!

ZEUS: Our problem is solved. The gods and goddesses are pleased. The citizens have spoken. Cecrops, announce the name of this new city.

CECROPS: Athena, a fine reward for you for bringing us such a gift! Our new city will be named Athens. We will build glorious temples and present you with treasure. We will have festivals. We will honor you, goddess of wisdom, for whom our city is named. (*Cecrops calls out.*) Athens! Our new city is to be called Athens!

CITIZENS: (*dancing around*) Athens! A great name for a new city!

Athena bows, and everyone applauds.

Respond to Reading

Summarize

Use details from the text to summarize *The Naming of Athens*. Your chart may help you.

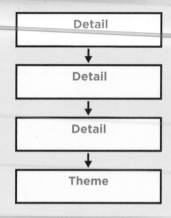

| Detail |
| Detail |
| Detail |
| Theme |

Text Evidence

1. How can you tell *The Naming of Athens* is a play and a myth? List two things that you notice about this kind of text. GENRE

2. What did the citizens think of the gifts Poseidon and Athena chose for the citizens? THEME

3. Find the word *powerful* on page 4. What is the root word of *powerful*? What do you think *powerful* means? ROOT WORDS

4. Write a version of the story in which Poseidon is the winner. What would be different? WRITE ABOUT READING

Compare Texts

Read how Luke finds a perfect present for his mother.

The Perfect Present

The day before Mom's birthday, I went with my dad to the mall. "I have no clue about what to buy for your mother!" Dad muttered.

I sighed and said, "I don't know what to get either. I've only got $5.50."

Dad told me that he could give me some money to add to my pocket money, but I like to be independent. "No thanks," I said.

Dad bought a shirt for Mom in a boutique, but I looked in all the shops and I couldn't find anything. I thought about making a card and getting a bar of soap.

When we stopped at the grocery store on the way home, I found a better present—one that I could afford. Strawberries!

"Good choice, son," said Dad as he eyed the strawberries. "Perhaps I should try one to see if they taste as good as they look!"

I laughed as I paid the cashier for the fresh berries. At home, I hurried up the stairs and hid the strawberries in my room. I made Mom a beautiful birthday card shaped like a strawberry, and then I went down to dinner.

Early the next morning I tiptoed down to the kitchen. I washed the strawberries and put them in a bowl.

"Happy Birthday, Mom," I said as I pushed open the bedroom door. I gave her the strawberries and the card.

Mom sat up and rubbed her eyes. "My favorite! How delicious! And what a gorgeous card!" she said.

"When you've finished the strawberries, I'll bring you some coffee," I said. Then I saw Dad's hand move.

"Watch out, Mom!" I yelled. "Dad is after your strawberries!"

"Well, if he helps you make the coffee, I might give him one," said Mom, laughing.

"You couldn't have gotten your mother a better present," said Dad as we made coffee.

I was pleased that Dad said that. I was pleased with myself, too. I think I did pretty well to find something special for Mom. Special and affordable!

Make Connections

In *The Perfect Present,* how did Luke decide what to buy for his mother? ESSENTIAL QUESTION

What helps the citizens in *The Naming of Athens* and Luke in *The Perfect Present* choose what they want? TEXT TO TEXT

Focus on Genre

Plays A play is a story that is written to be performed rather than read. The people who perform in a play are called actors. Sets show the audience where the action is taking place. Props, such as the olive tree in *The Naming of Athens,* also help make the story come alive.

Read and Find In *The Naming of Athens,* the names of the characters are written in upper case and bold. A colon separates the name of the character from the words that the character will speak. The stage directions are written in italics. These directions tell the actors what to do.

Your Turn

Imagine if another god, such as Apollo, the god of the sun, also entered the competition. What gift might he have offered? Write your ideas as another scene for *The Naming of Athens.* Remember to use text features to show which character is speaking and what the character is saying and doing.